A Testament of Witnesses and Other Poems

A TESTAMENT OF WITNESSES AND OTHER POEMS

Copyright © 2022 David Lyle Jeffrey. All rights reserved. Except for brief quotations in critical publications or reviews, no part of this book may be reproduced in any manner without prior written permission from the publisher. Write: Permissions, Wipf and Stock Publishers, 199 W. 8th Ave., Suite 3, Eugene, OR 97401.

Resource Publications
An Imprint of Wipf and Stock Publishers
199 W. 8th Ave., Suite 3
Eugene, OR 97401

www.wipfandstock.com

PAPERBACK ISBN: 978-1-6667-3762-2
HARDCOVER ISBN: 978-1-6667-9728-2
EBOOK ISBN: 978-1-6667-9729-9

A Testament of Witnesses
and Other Poems

David Lyle Jeffrey

RESOURCE *Publications* · Eugene, Oregon

Table of Contents

Preface vii
Acknowledgments ix
Prolegomena: Shaphan the Scribe 1
The Isaiah Cantos: A Prophet and His Readers 5
    Nechamu 6
    Nechamu Ami 7
    Yeshayahu 9
    Sofer, a Scribe 10
    Shimshai, Sofer 11
    Ezra, Sofer b'Yisroel 12
    Ben Sira the Younger 15
    James the Lesser 17
    Luke, Physician 19
Ezekiel: Last Will and Testament 25
Jonah, Recalcitrant Prophet 32
Mary I 36
Skywatchers and Scholars 37
Mary II 40
John the Baptist (a Pharisee Reports) 41
A Marginal Man 42
A Centurion 43
Descendants of Abraham 44
Blessed are the Poor in Spirit 45
Zacchaeus 46
Mark 48
Christ Crucified 49
A Temple Guard 50
Magdalene Remembers 51

Table of Contents

Pentecost I 52
Pentecost II 53
Gamaliel 55
To Timothy: A Postscript 56
John on Patmos 57

Miscellaneous Poems 58
Christ on the Cross 59
The Cross 60
Blessed are the Meek 61
Quaecumque sunt Vera 62
On Handel's *Coronation Anthem* 63
Advent I 64
Advent II 65
Advent III 66
Advent IV 67
Christmas Eve, 2021 68
Nod: A Child's Hebrew Lesson 69
On Psalm 119:105 70
Persuasion 71
Yang's Gift 72
Reviewing my Latest Chinese Banquet 73
Everyday Valentines 75
Snowdrift 76
Of Life to Come 77
Recipe for Insomnia 78
About Kalypso 79
Telemachus 80
La petite voisine d'Essoyes 81
October 82
Misreading 83
Confession 84
Just a Toast at Twilight 85
Somnium 86
September Rain 87
Bittersweet 88
Azura 89
Snow Geese 90
Migrating Water Birds 91
Arc of the Covenants 92

Preface

THE TITLE OF THIS volume of poems, as many readers will have sensed, draws in part upon the admonition of the writer to the Hebrews (Heb. 12:1). It is in the nature of biblical narrative that, so far from being prolix, it is terse, focusing on essentials. The gaps in the stories, places where we wish to know more, invite wonder about those ancient persons who were in such direct contact with the workings of plot and Providence. As a child I found myself trying to imagine what it might be like to hear the voice of God in person, audibly, or to witness his actions. What about those who heard, saw, and yet refused? What did they think? And how did the words of Jesus strike the hearts of those who were wooed by him, who followed, who came to deep belief? My biblical poems, mostly dramatic monologue by genre, are in this way thought experiments. I am not trying to answer—as if such answers would be helpful to anyone else—the question, "What does this mean to me?"

The Miscellaneous poems added here are, on the other hand, mostly personal reflections, though there are also a few whimsical items written for children.

DLJ, March 8, 2022

Acknowledgments

A FEW OF THESE poems have previously appeared in magazines. I am grateful to their editors for permission to reprint them here. "A Marginal Man" and "Christmas, 2021" appeared first in *Forward in Christ*; "Magdalene Remembers," "Bittersweet," "*Quaecumque sunt Vera*," and "Arc of the Covenants" in *Faith Today*; "Christ Crucified" in *Crossings*; and "Snow Geese" in *Local Culture*. All other poems appear here for the first time.

Prolegomena: Shaphan the Scribe

Like father, like son they said of Amon,
But less than two years in his wicked reign
He seemed to be worse than old Manasseh. On
Suppositions such he was surprised and slain,
Slaughtered by servants in his own latrine. They fain
Would make a brigand king, disdaining prior claim.

Such was Judah in those days, sick to the bone and soul. Bel,
Asherah, and Moloch, idols everywhere, defied the One true God
Of Moses and King David. Lust, murder, sacrilege—who could tell,
Or even wish to know the horrors of those awful times? The sod
Was drenched in blood, babies burnt alive, their mothers screaming;
That sickening sacrament of sex and death drowned out all pleading.

The conspirators were seized and slain in turn. Again alone
And headless, Judah lay open then to worse abuse. At once
We named the first-born son of Amon successor to the throne,
Little knowing if Josiah too would prove wicked or a dunce;
He was but eight years old, conceived when Amon was fifteen
Upon one of the women seized to serve his lust and preen

Their appetite for darker deeds. This one of that inglorious lot
Was not to lechery bent, but faithful, daughter of Zion sent
Into our valley of death, as now we know, to prepare for respite, not
Corrupt, but mercifully neglected once her child was born. She spent
Years on her own. Jedediah raised her 'Lemuel' lad and taught him well
Enough that even as a boy of eight his virtue shone and none could tell

He was his father's child. Out of her seclusion he was called to rule
And needed help. His mother sought a faithful priest and me
To teach him script and writ; we went through *tehellim*, his only school
But for his mother's wisdom, *mashalim*. To both Josiah took; they were to be
His cast of mind and depth of thought, the manner of his talk and walk
Through youth and later years. In time the scoffers ceased to mock.

At twenty-six he acted boldly on his own, sent to Hilkiah, high priest,
To bid the Temple treasury be opened, willing workers thither brought
To clear and clean, restore the ruin of war and dereliction; the least
Object to be re-made as perfect as before. In that work Josiah sought
No fine account of money spent for stone or timber. Worthy of their hire
his servants were; to nothing more than serve the king did they aspire.

What followed next was not foreseen. Assyrians, pleasing pagan gods, saw
Our altars each defiled, destroyed our scrolls long since, or so we thought,
But in a blocked-up niche, wrapped in dusty shrouds, the sacred Book of Law
Was found. Hilkiah quickly brought it out and bade me read. Whoever thought
That such a revelation could again be ours? I shook with joy and, yes, with fear,
Knowing that the word within was urgent news, and that the king himself must
    hear.

Without delay, he asked me then to read the words before him on that day,
And read I did, with awe and trembling in my voice. He heard with wide-eyed
    wonder
At the first, and then with groans and tears. At these words he wept, yet heard
    me say
"They are a nation void of counsel, nor is any understanding in them. Oh, that
    under
My wrath they had grown wise enough to consider well their final end." That
    read,
He tore his clothes, cried out for shame, fell down upon the ground and pled

That I should stop until he caught his breath—then prayed aloud for mercy for us all.
Not merely thus informed, his heart was transformed by the word of God. At once
He acted, sending me, Abba Hilkiah, Ahikam, Achbor, and Asaiah, forthwith to call
On Huldah, prophetess, since Jeremiah was far off, away among the exiled ones.
We asked for counsel from the Lord about our fate. Nothing contradicting Moses
Did she say, or Jeremiah either, but that Josiah's true repentance grace discloses,

Mercy in his case. Thence to work. Josiah gathered all together in the proper place,
With prophets, priests, and servants of the crown, himself read out the sacred Book,
The law God gave to Moses, every word, bid everyone repent and turn his face
Away from evil to the Lord. The people then as one the Covenant affirmed, nor looked
At images and high places now except to burn them and deface the same, every stain
Removing, idols ground to powder, ash and dust. All this was done; the Word was plain.

Josiah served the Lord, heart, soul and strength—this none could then or now deny.
My task was just to bear due witness, testify to what transpired; I had a pen.
Yet ponder this: God's Law when kept can turn foul fortune back, can grace supply,
As this tale shows, yet blessings more were also there, already given in the Law. Then
Harken to the Lord, I say; he knows us better than we do, so seek withal to understand.
As Samuel to Saul once said, obedience is best; God's wrath no mortal may withstand.

The Isaiah Cantos:
A Prophet and his Readers

Nechamu
on Isaiah 40:1

The word is comfort. Second person plural,
Imperative verb. Not to be misunderstood.
It doesn't mean 'relax' or, 'take it easy someplace rural',
But implies instead a future city one could
Just about imagine, and though far off, still
Guaranteed, a promise yet to be fulfilled.

In time, in this terrestrial space
All flesh shall, trembling, see the Lord.
His captive chosen, those who face
Again a long exile, heard here a word
Not just for them but for their seed,
That remnant who his final Word will heed.

Finding solace in a future good meant
Not for now but generations yet to come
Requires more than faith; inspired love sent
Out to those unborn prompts hope for some
Whose faces we can't see, indeed, for Jews
Who Abram saw far off, but God alone did choose.

Nechamu Ami

After the cruel hooks and ropes, mile after mile
Stumbling along desert roads, each day
A torture, watching the sick cut loose, the file
Plodding on past bleeding bodies; each to stay
Where it fell till the vultures came—
No jeering soldier's whip brought greater pain.

It's a long haul from Jerusalem to Babylon plain.
Those who made it strove to forget the warnings stark
With which the prophets tried to coax us back again
To God, his clear *mitzvot*, his *piqquidim* not dark
Or hard to understand—we knew, but hated so—
Lust, luxury, and fashion were all we wished to know.

Generations come and go. We've languished here so long
We've blended in; new gods, new names and dress.
By Israel's God since then abandoned, our collective wrong
Supposed the cause. *Lo ami* now to him, we repress
For shame our fathers' names, the covenant claim that then
Entailed we worshipped El—not Bel—with harp and voice and pen.

There is a poet in this town who kept his Hebrew name
And prays to our fathers' God. His songs are sung
By youngsters tagging after him; his fame
Is such they made a scroll, the title flung
Around as if *Yeshayahu* yet could be revealed.
It begins, "Comfort ye my people," nor is it sealed—

As if it were a finished book. The poet is old,
A scruffy fellow, poorly dressed. He sings
Along our shtetl streets, warm days or cold,
Even when mocked; he claims he brings
Good news to the poor, that our children shall return
To Zion, singing Hebrew songs he helps them learn.

Such fantasies are dangerous, a fruitless hope
At best. It's a wonder some satrap hasn't run him through
With a hot blade. His crazy cry might seem a slippery slope
To insurrection.   Perhaps his thick, poetic old Hebrew
Obscures. Like all prophets he claims his speech
Is not his own, but God's. That hardly puts him out of reach.

Still, I find myself awake at night, worrying if what he says is true.
What if Elohenu yet pursues? Still regards us as his people?
Our children might yet see the place, Jerusalem renew?
Hananiah, Azariah, Mishael, Daniel, and sad Ezekiel
Likewise say: 'Still he stretches out his hand to those who seek'
—Not to the mighty, mind you, but the meek.

Yeshayahu

Yes, but I am not the One for whom you look
In all the wrong places. Once my lips were seared
With that hot coal from the altar fire, the angel took
Away my voice; now what I speak is not my own. I feared
To get it wrong, but needn't. The One who speaks just fills my head
At night with words so strong my heart grows faint. I rise from bed

As if on fire, quick to get it said or sung while I have breath
And there are ears to hear it. These ones who follow, door to door,
Ensure the words are kept. Now I am approaching death
And fear that not at all. The One who called me is far more
To me than life. His Word is life, goes on and out forever.
Though all kingdoms fall; from him no foe can sever.

I had two sons whose names were omens. Until she died
The prophetess and they alone knew how weary
I came home at night, soul-spent, no matter how I tried
Incapable of chit-chat. In candle-light my eyes grew bleary;
Soon I shall be blind. My work for the Lord is almost done.
They are making a scroll, writing it down for those to come.

Sofer, a Scribe

As you can see, I am a scribe. Like all my guild I work for hire,
Glad of employment; by day I meekly serve "the great king,"
As foolishly they call him. At night I serve a Greater, do not tire
But with others who have heard God's prophet sing, I bring
His poems to written form. We help each other, pray
For precision, revise until we have it right, no thought of pay.

This is our true vocation. We know that *teudah* voice
Is not for comfort we shall know, but for God's people yet unborn.
We work to get it down. Though we die here, they shall rejoice
In Judah, says our God. There is no use in grumbling now, forlorn,
When those ransomed of the Lord shall yet return to Zion, singing
Perhaps these very songs, with joyful hearts their voices ringing

Praises for his kingdom come, faithful servants then to hold
To sacred vows, the Covenant in full obedience renew
And children's children taught again the Word, brought to the fold
From which our people stray like errant sheep when priests eschew
Their call to find and lead them home. The prophet sings of grace,
And not for us alone, but all who seek it, every tribe and race.

Shimshai, Sofer

When we saw they had come back, more than forty thousand strong
And hundreds of horses, we were alarmed. Had the great Cyrus
Lost his mind? The message we crafted was more tactful: "By us,
O mighty King, and so forth—to let this herd of Jews return was wrong,
For they are a rebellious lot and will cause trouble."

Just when it looked like we were making progress, Cyrus died.
We had to deal with Darius, who shocked us by holding
To his predecessor's word. All the while the walls enfolding
Jerusalem were restored. We did our best to stop it, tried
Threats of violence by night and even random murder.

Those damned Judeans are as quick as crafty. In fifty-two days
The walls were up, and that rascal Nehemiah laying down the Law.
Ezra his scribe, I must admit, no mere counter of letters, oversaw
Translation of Moses into the common tongue. The way he prays
Is like unto a priest of old, or that prophet we thought safely dead.

Ezra, Sofer b'Yisroel

This day has been the apex of my life: inside these walls
To read aloud *ha davarim* in the hearing of all.
At the *parsha* "and teach them"—that no precept falls
Into the pit of forgetfulness, so each generation recalls
His greatness and his mercy—my tears welled up, voice cracked
Before my *yad* could reach "voice from the fire." I lacked

Due scribal distance from the text, and was as chastened there
On hearing the deeds of the Lord as anyone. When Moishe told
How we were brought "out of Egypt's iron furnace," no hair
Singed, to be his people, I smiled to think of Mishael's bold
Faith before *his* fiery furnace, but read on, the old Hebrew
Parsed quickly by my students, as they the meaning drew

Out in Aramaic, the common, crude commercial speech
Of Babylon, the only language most now knew. Chosen of God
Should in better accents, purer diction speak; learn, reach
Back to words once given where the sense is clear. We nod
To necessity though, since simple understanding will suffice
For walking in the way commanded, lest ignorance pay the price

Of disobedience. The great *Sh'ma* marks the first corrective step;
Love is the key to it. By late morning, while I read, "This day,
Hayyom hazzeh, you are again the people of the Lord," men wept,
Swept up in joy of our redemption. When they heard me say
Aloud those *adah* threats, captivity to come, the cost
And consequence of faithlessness, some tore their robes, lost

All composure. But when we came to "courage," the call
To turn to God with all our hearts, that, having heard, the word
Might come again into our mouths, confessing each and all
Belong to God, that there is nothing in His Law the least absurd
Or daunting, I heard the crowd before me say a loud "Amen"
From willing hearts, keen to make things right, to name his Name again.

Some thought they saw in the crowd a Samaritan spy
Attent to the targum Zechariah was giving his lot,
Pretending to be one of us. Likely that man was Shimshai,
A scribe I knew from the school in Babylon. He thought it not
Seemly that our master scrivener should set a decree
Of once-mad Nebuchadnezzar as our copy text, how his mind came free,

And reason returned when he looked up, confessing that our Lord is God.
In that class of twenty most were Chaldee through and through,
But three of us were Jews and he, a Gentile mixed, risked the rod
By mocking up his sleeve. Our teacher, likewise a Jew,
Was well regarded by the court, thus appointed to his task.
By night he was our Mishael, laying aside his courtly mask.

As one of those who heard and marked the songs
Of *Yeshayahu*, greatest of our prophets, he put his trust
In the poetry of God, certain we would return in throngs
Singing their beauty back in praise, though for himself he must
Remain, he said, curator for the king by day, scrivener by night
Of the prophet's latter poems, determined to get the words just right,

Recorded true to God's own voice. Today we have begun,
But there will come a better, for in his time
The Lord of Glory will himself appear, and what was won
This day seem then mere shadow, dress rehearsal, sign
That God will come in person to his waiting Israel,
As in those songs of promise, be to us Emmanuel.

Ben Sira the Younger

Our fathers wandered here,
Weary of the endless wars
And rumors of impending doom.
Some came for learning,
Some for looser living—
Some for both.

My *saba*'s text was written
To keep alive the wisdom of our Book.
He wrote in Hebrew, not despising
Greek, but sure that Plato
And Aristotle's ilk lacked something
That to us was spoken also in God's deeds.

It is a kind of summary, lest we forget
To honor what is ours alone—
Or was before we lost our hope
In the coming of the Kingdom.
To wisdom then he added plot,
Recalled the famous names.

I've set it now in Greek,
But as in my preface I relate,
Much is lost, not least the poetry.
My grandfather, a man of the Book,
Would doubtless be displeased,
But what can we do? So few know Hebrew.
I remember him stooped by his lamp,
Reading the prophet called Isaiah,

The one who "showed what should come
To pass forever, and secret things e're ever
They came," as he put it. To the end of his days
He wondered at those things yet to be.

"When and how," he'd ask, "shall these things
Come to pass? What Jews will live to see it?"
I wonder too, and wait for understanding still.
From Alexandria's flowered streets, Jerusalem is remote;
Many have forgotten all. Perhaps his wisdom book
Now turned to Greek will help restore our Jewish story.

James the Lesser

Yes, I am called James, but small wonder you are confused;
With so many named for old Jacob that tags are used
To tell us apart. I am 'Wee James,' nor much abused
By it, for as you see, *naim* I am, *mikros* as you Greeks say.

Also I am "the brother of the Lord" to some
Because of Him whose life to learn you come.
We were family, worked together in the shop; in sum
Shared daily bread. We walked to synagogue that day.

He had been gone for several weeks. Abba Joseph knew,
But kept his stepson's doings private, smiled and grew
Pensive when we asked. "He must now other work pursue
Than ours," he'd say, "another call he must obey."

As is our custom, we stood to hear the word.
The cantor led us in a psalm, the twenty-third,
And then the leader called on him. As if a bird
Flew in, the air around us stirred; he rose to pray.

He took the *navi'im* scroll in hand, opened at one end,
To where Isaiah speaks of One who God would send:
"The spirit of the Lord God is upon me," souls to mend,
Captives redeem, sickness cure, comfort, wrongs repay.

There was a power in his reading; all who heard
Trembled with anticipation, grateful for the soothing word
Of promise. Until, that is, he said what seemed absurd,
That even as he read it was fulfilled—he meant in him—that day.

When they realized what his midrash meant, men were enraged.
Even we brothers, though often by his cryptic speech engaged
Before, were stunned. Claiming to be the Lord's Anointed presaged
The inevitable, a charge of blasphemy. Many witnessed, thought to slay

Him then and there—and almost did. How he got away
I still don't know. Next Sabbath we brothers feared going back to pray.

Luke, Physician

Strange though it must seem to a fellow Greek,
I went to Judah seeking wisdom. True enough,
I took on physician's work, but not to seek
Wealth. The ship was old, the passage rough.

Insatiable for learning from our classic sages,
In early years I devoured books of Plato, Plotinus,
Aristotle and more. With us, I thought, wisdom for the ages
Reigns supreme—of Athens' glory yet reminds us.

But Athens fell. Wherein did our wisdom fail?
I read a Jewish book called *Solomon's Wisdom*,
Quite by chance. In Greek. Intrigued, I soon set sail
Hoping to learn how wisdom there connects to health, *shalom*.

In Jerusalem I read more books—Moses and the Prophet
Chiefly. I found a synagogue which welcomed me,
And since I shared their loathing of Moloch and Tophet
They urged me to convert, become a 'Jew-to-be.'

I agreed, for the more I learned the Hebrew tongue,
The more of their books I read in it as well as Greek,
The deeper seemed their ancient bards who sung
The healing mercies of their God, his blessings on the meek.

For me that was one great difference—care for the weak
Is essential to their thought. Another point: fear
Of the One God is key for one who would seek
Wisdom, for only in holy reverence can one hear.

"Faith comes by hearing," I heard one say.
"And hearing by the Word of God." Here then
A precept, that attending to this wisdom may
Result in faith in things unseen as yet by men,

But such as may come true. The Prophet in his time
Saw not, but gave the startling word that there would be
A birth some day in Judah that no science, coarse or fine,
Has ever conjured: son to a virgin born, a king to set them free.

One of the teachers I met, a Pharisee of good fame,
Responding to questions about one who had claimed to be king.
Said that this man, crucified by Pilate, Jesus by name.
Occasioned new disputes, "for among us are some that bring

Stories of his death and reported resurrection to bear
On understanding Scriptures concerning He who is to come."
He meant the *Moshiach*. "Such fables don't wear
Well," he said, "yet correspondences are found among

The Scriptures to his peculiar life and tortured death."
I enquired of these matters in detail, learned of blind
Men cured, lame and lepers too that still drew breath,
Their cures witnessed by priests judged sound of mind.

Remembering Isaiah, on some of these I went to call
As a physician, looking to see where the evidence led.
Marvel upon marvel upon my eyes and ears did fall,
I tell you truly. A woman said, "twelve years I bled and bled.

None of your kind could help, no matter what I paid.
Not even seeing me—I merely touched his robe—he healed
Just like that, without a word! and scarce his footsteps stayed.
Yet turning, kindly said my faith had healed me, sealed

My wound forever, then walked on. As if no credit was to him!"
I kept a notebook, and witness after witness likewise set down.
One led me to another. I met finally a brother, close of kin,
James Mikros, small of stature, amusing fellow, now renowned.

He told me how Jeshua, asked at their synagogue to read,
Chose the scroll, a passage from Isaiah, "the Spirit of the Lord,
Has appointed me to preach good news to those in need,
To heal the brokenhearted"; they took it as a welcome word

Until he said, "Today this Scripture is fulfilled in your hearing."
At that they tried to kill him for blasphemy, almost succeeded,
And that was but the beginning. Galileans fearing
God then came to him in throngs; his followers pleaded

For more teaching, tagged along to synagogues around the lake
And listened, sometimes in great numbers when outside he taught,
Watching amazed as he cured the halt and blind, only to make
The crowds still larger, such were the wonders that he wrought.

There was talk of his strange birth as well; to a virgin appeared
An angel, announcing his advent as the Promised One of old.
Some believed it; some not. James said his mother feared
Her time was almost gone, but believed Isaiah had foretold

Her destiny, to bear a son whose name should be Emmanuel.
"Now He has died and risen; we know with whom we woke
And worked was not a man like us, nor yet like Samuel
Or Elijah, but that Servant of whom David and Isaiah spoke."

"If his mother—yours?—yet lives, might she be willing to speak
With me?" I asked. He showed me to their simple home
And what that gracious lady told me was such as men may seek
Forever and not find. She sung to me her Hebrew poem

In a clear, soft voice. She had been at his Cross when He died.
Entrusted to John, who loved her as a son, she kept in her heart
Many things, then came to see Isaiah's Suffering Servant, tried
And slain for other's sins, as her Redeemer, and knew her part.

Despised and rejected, man of sorrows, acquainted with grief.
"They got it wrong," she said, "thought him one more mere crucified
Victim of fate. But 'wounded for our transgressions,' not a thief.
He was the sacrificial lamb for all, so God's eternal justice satisfied."

All that the prophet spoke of Him had proven true
In Jerusalem and Judah, as foretold. This was the greater healing,
Transcending all I sought to learn in books or thought I knew.
My search was over. Mind filled, my heart was reeling

With the way of it. My least suspected was One long expected
by those who read Isaiah, heard in those poems a higher voice,
Bore witness to prophecy fulfilled, thus, through One rejected
By those He came to heal, found health itself, and still rejoice.

Ezekiel: Last Will and Testament

Would that it had been just a bad dream,
But alas, it was the Lord who made me look.
Where Jewish eyes might well expect a gleam
Of holy light; none shone within that dark, no book
Of God was there, no prayer, just horror stark
And blatant profanation—no mere missing of the mark.

I

Outside he showed the Temple I once served.
It seemed the home I longed for still, until I saw, set
By the north gate of the inner court, the goddess. Unnerved,
By that sculpted form of female beauty lent to lust, yet
Loathe to speak its shameful name, 'image of jealousy' wrote,
For jealousy among our women was its purpose to promote

As much as lust among the men. What made this outrage worse,
The Glory of the Lord beside me still flamed out in gold,
Bright as noonday sun; its radiant heat like a sudden curse
Fell like lightening on the sculpted stone. Alas, that idol told
But the beginning. He took me to the wall, a hidden door,
Looked into a secret room; priests and scribes sat on the floor

As if to study Torah, learning to read and heed the Law of God.
Not so. There hunched now the seventy, Ja'aziniah in the middle,
And he, though son of righteous Shaphan, seemed to nod
As if approving every greasy self-caress, each man a-diddle,
Each locked in some chamber of his own fantasy, impervious
To filth and profanation, of vile, grotesque perversity oblivious.

I shuddered to see, in place of priestly Torah training
Rank sacrilege—worship of reptiles, nature, ritual sex—
Disdaining the Maker of all, whilst outside wailing
Women weeping for Tammuz, god of faux fertility, did vex
My spirit further for the house of God blasphemed. Shocked,
I wondered what should follow; God is not thus mocked

Indefinitely. Then out from the Presence came a piercing call,
Six warriors, each with a battle axe, appeared; my belly shook
With fear. A seventh, cloaked in linen, had a writer's kit; stern and tall
Like my old master scribe, he carried pen and ink, yet no book.
His charge seemed odd—that he write *tov* on foreheads of those
Alone who decried the evil, who God and not the Temple chose.

Immediately the other six were sent to follow that strange scribe
And strike down everyone on whom no forehead *tov* was found;
Swiftly they did it, sparing not for age or sex or class or tribe,
Till bodies lay all over streets and Temple, scattered round
Like fallen leaves. I cried for mercy on the Chosen, Abraham's kin;
He answered: "those are mine who love my Law, abhorring sin."

Wherewith the glory of his Presence seemed to move, shift
Out from cherub's wings through the *devir*, out to the portal,
Where it paused. I held my breath—was terrified to see it lift
With cherubim above the Temple roof, rising beyond all mortal
View, up and through the clouds, leaving below just empty air
In the dusty court. The Glory had departed! Despair! Despair!

II

Never wish to be a prophet of the Lord. Never seek or pretend to such
Appointing, for all imposters are already damned. There is no school
For prophets, just a Call. None who heed the Lord's command much
Like what follows—sting and scorn, mocking and curses. No fool
Would choose these least of sorrows; far worse, rejection and defeat.
He who serves must truly self-efface, the words of God alone repeat

Or pantomime, as in my case, bodily contortions, awkward, long
To bear, with no response but mockery, nor respite, just the goad
Of God that if I did not bear him witness in *his* way I would be wrong,
Responsible for Israel's blood and damnèd souls. Take another road
Than this if you wish mortal fame. God's prophet has no choice
But following the script—no path here to 'finding your own voice.'

III

The fate of Ja'azaniah and Pelatiah made clear another point;
Though sins of fathers are visited on their offspring,
The faithfulness of none can be bequeathed. A soul out of joint,
Though child of Noah, Daniel, or Job, shall die—in vain bring
Sacrifice to the altar. He holds each to account for his own sins,
Spares each alike for personal *zedekah*. No successor wins

His mercy through a family name or proxy. So by like token,
His Presence in the Temple is of no avail when inward hearts
Of those who enter play with idols. God has plainly spoken,
And he will act according to his word. When the Presence starts
Up from the Ark, leaves the *devir*, he will not tarry; the sinner's plea
Will be too late, prophet and priest will plead in vain on bended knee.

Truth engenders hate. None would admit that the Glory had departed;
Apostates feign faith when the jig is up. My job was still to say
So, and repeat it. Those furious elders shut their ears, spit hard-hearted
Insults. Their fate who heard me thus declared, not one turned to pray
For mercy; most cursed the holy Name. My painful labors largely lost,
My witness vain, I wept. Who would follow, let him count the cost.

IV

Anguish! O anguish for my people! Raise voice and cry
Mercy for fools, the obdurate, the little children slain!
Yet mercy will not come, for they still scorn, nor reason why
Their misery deepens; each day's steep decline deny, maintain
Their habitude of death, abjure remorse, decry belief, ply
Wares of devils' craft and devils' purse that no life can sustain
Or even slow the bleeding, stint the bile. They'd rather die
Than seek the truth, live out each lie than greed and lust restrain.

What shall I say to you, Jerusalem, that I have not said?
Ungrateful for mercies, who every gift usurps: self-glory!
Indulge, indulge! Go on—devour your seed, their daily bread.
Revel in your puerile games! Revile the pure! The dismal story
You helped write, though never thought to hear or read,
Now nears the end you chose, your doom, no matter how you plead.

V

God hardens hearts of willful rebels; so, in quite another way,
The heart of this old battered prophet. Grim repetition, endless scorn,
Parable on parable fell on deaf ears; I, no matter what parlay,

He bade me more, more upon more, yet still they raised their horn
In wrath. And then he made of me a broken sign, of her bereaved,
My heart's desire, nor even let me mourn; my task was unrelieved.

Not mere gesture, but felt participation in his grief for the city
Far off in measure, not in mind, first joy of every Jewish heart.
Much more vain-hopeful Judah, now to be slain without pity
Who thought the walls secure enough, unable to imagine their part
In the coming judgment of an angry God. And swiftly then it came
Just as he said. Those oracles on Tyre and Sidon, portend the same.

VI

You may imagine the shame of it, though not perhaps his fury.
The Lord was relentless, insisting that each judgment be pronounced
In full detail. I mind less his wrath upon the nations, nor worry
About their fate, but my spirit sank with each decree announced
On Judah and Jerusalem. Just as I was yearning for some slender hope
Word came: the city had fallen, come to the end of its fraying rope.

Then he spoke to me again, loosened my tongue to speak his wrath
Upon the shepherds, priests, and keepers of his flock who smote
The sheep, abused and fed them poison, barring entrance to the path
Of holiness and health, rejecting life, performing dumb, dull rote
Their sacred altar rites. And yet, though selfish hirelings flout
Their duty to his flock, God himself will spare a remnant, will rout

False shepherds, replace them with a true and greater on that day.
His servant David, he has said, by mystery then shall reappear
To guard and keep, to gather in the scattered sheep, their fretful way
Make safe for evermore. I did not understand, yet to my eyes a tear

Came as he spoke, again as I repeated him in turn, and even now when
I retell it quietly to you. O think what glad rejoicing will be then!

Again he bade me prophesy, not this time to stony hearts of men
But Judah's stony mountains, proclaiming that he will restore
The land itself one day, give fruitfulness like that of Eden,
That nations all around shall know that he is Lord. And more,
He set me in a valley strewn with dead, dry bones of many slain
And had me prophesy to them! And bone to bone reknit again

And tendons, flesh alike appeared and skin until there stood
Before me a great host. For people of Israel now of hope bereft,
To those already turned to dust, he lent breath and spoke good
News: 'Behold I will raise them from their graves, dust left
Of Israel and of Judah, and I shall join them, form one holy stock
Again, put over them King David, good shepherd of my flock.'

VII

At this I something understood, and wished the story ended there.
Even mountains and dead bones now knew what living men refused,
Yet *El Shaddai* had more, warnings for nations far away from where
He brought his people, and still his chosen would restore, transfused
With his own Spirit, holy, prosperous, at peace with nations near,
Yet prideful, war-like tribes far north will plot in envy, nor God fear.

Why should the whole world hate us? Because they hate the God
Who chose us out of all nations to be his treasured people, chose
Us his love and glory to reveal. As other men have aimless trod
So walked we too before he cut our covenant, gave his law to those
He led by Moses up from darkness into light. Thus, as we now turn
Toward his promised Sabbath rest, we find *shalom* which others spurn.

VIII

For many years his silence meant reprieve; I did common work.
Then that voice fell on me once again, though not to command
Some new declamation of his coming wrath. Nothing did I shirk,
But he, of his mercy showed me visions of the future he has planned
Long since, a new Jerusalem, a new and greater Temple in detail.
He had me set it down. Each angle and dimension must prevail
In times to come. I saw, I heard, I wrote it all, of courtyard, altar,
Doors and wall, of holy place and priesthood called, of holy duty done
By holy hands. The gates were twelve, the portals wide. Nothing alter
In the plan, for it is his. Let no wit or man's devising change it—none!
I there beheld his Glory, Israel's God through Eastgate come,
His voice like roaring waters sang; all shone around him like the sun.

So real it was that my heart danced, mistaking that he came to reign.
"Let now this gate be shut," he said, "that none may enter till
The God of Israel comes again to claim his Temple and his Name
Set once more on Mt. Zion, then all this land with blessing fill."

Your task now my friend? to see this scroll kept safe till near that day
When faithful men shall need it to rebuild. Do not fail me, pray.
My breath is coming harder now, my heart beats slow and skips.
The word he gave through all my life is rolled up there; share
With none but faithful folk and bid them guard it well. Who grips
The purport will not doubt that God has spoken. Let not your care
Diminish! *Yahweh shammah*! The Lord is there! and will be there
       forever.

Jonah, Recalcitrant Prophet
(cf. Matt. 12:41)

OK, I admit it. I messed things up in spectacular style.
But this much extenuate: it's an ugly culture on Ninevah plain;
After all, from the judgment of the Lord himself while
Sending me there, who could doubt he thought the same?

Look—I am a fairly fastidious Jew; I keep to the Law
Mostly. Those Ninnies eat pig, and slimy bottom feeders too!
Where to get good kosher nosh? That stuck in my Jewish craw.
Why preach at butt-ugly pagans till my face turned blue?

He was set to destroy them after all. If Jews won't repent, I thought,
Why would they? How to escape this loathsome task to hand?
Get out of *Ha Shem*'s jurisdiction! So I went to the port and bought
Passage to Tarshish, far off to the west, fleeing the Lord's command.

Why there? Ah, let me tell you about Tarshish. Rich, urbane,
Très chic. The cafés there have world-renown, serve
Fabled wines and sherbets steeped in gin; no other claim
To culinary glory matches theirs. "To Tarshish then, nor swerve

From your course," I said to the captain of our galley ship.
"On vacation?" he smiled and took my fare. Our journey well
Begun, my hopes were high. Then gusts of wind seemed like to tip
Us over. Skies drew dark, down came the sails. Wave swell

Knocked us about. I went below in hope of sleep. Then rudely awoke
With the captain shaking me. The storm was worse, the ship in distress;
I could hear men crying out to various gods. The captain spoke,
"Call upon your god if you have one. Do you? Then rise and address

That god—be quick!" Alas for me, I knew right then what was amiss.
The sailors huddled in the stern, casting lots to see whose fault;
I knew it would point to me—and it did. "Who in the name of Dis
Are you? Why are you here?" Looking up at the black and roiling vault

Above, I confessed: "I am a Jew. My God is Creator of heaven and earth,
And he is angry with me because I am fleeing his command. So throw me
Out—the storm will cease. It isn't you he wants to drown. He has no dearth
Of reasons in my case." They resisted, first tossing their cargo into the sea.

That helped nothing, so with prayers in their teeth, they threw me in.
Amidst the waves I thought, "At least I won't have to see that pagan bunch,"
Then suddenly was grabbed by a great stinking fish, big as Leviathan!
I thought, "Drowning's not enough for the Lord: a sea monster's lunch

He prefers? Ah well, suffocating in fish guts shouldn't take long."
Wrong again. That fish kept coming up for gulps of air. Oy vey!
I was still lying in the slimy darkness and breathing stench in misery, long
After I should have been dead. Lacking a better idea, I ventured to pray.

Remembering a psalm that seemed apt, I began, "Out of the depths O Lord,"
I promised I would, if I could, make sacrifice at any altar I could reach,
Unlikely as were the odds from thence. But he heard. Nowhere to board
A boat, but after three days the great fish barfed me up on a foreign beach.

Deliverance by the hand of the Lord can take weird turns, but this was insult;
Doubtless he enjoyed it. Once rinsed of the kelp and stink I went upshore
Till I met a man cutting reeds. "Pardon, but where am I?" The gruff result
Was foreign speech but clear enough: the road to Ninevah. What's more,

He looked and laughed. "You look like a dog's breakfast, second round.
Why are *you* here?" That did it; I blew my stack. "To tell you this:

In forty days Nineveh, man and beast, will be kaput. Like the sound
Of that? Israel's God has fixed your doom unless you repent! Now piss

Off!" Such encounters, repeated often over the next few miles,
Made me hotter, till those I spoke to looked increasingly alarmed
And scurried off to warn others. After the city gate they came in files
Street by street, not to mock, but in sackcloth to wail lest they be harmed.

Their king himself was struck with fear. So he repented already, made a law
That all should fast, even the animals, bewail their many sins and call
On God to note their busy hustle of contrition. "Let there be no flaw
In our repentance," he said, "do the whole shtick. Omit zip. Do all!"

Forty days came and went. No fire fell, no plague swept their streets.
I couldn't believe it. God relented! The Ninevites rejoiced. I was furious.
Prophets in Israel preach forty years and *nobody* repents. That meets
with all the consequences. Lord! Being chosen means this? Er—just curious."

I slunk out of the city, loathe to watch slap-happy Ninevites a minute more,
Sat near a shrub and kvetched all night. In the morning a green gourd plant
Sprang up and gave me better shade. "God by his chosen sets no store,"
I said to myself, then wham, the gourd dried up and died. I began to rant,

"Why *them*, Eternal One? You called them rot yourself—unholy, vile!
Why should Dagon-worshipping, foul *goyim* be spared your holy wrath?
Their god's a *fish*! Ahhh—how choice, to deliver me up that way, while
Making me go where I wouldn't go, do what I would not do! What a path!

Good God! What now? You stoop to save even their stinking hogs?
Have you no respect for Torah? for Moses? His text is clear: don't eat!
At this rate all our rules will be crap; your people will go to the dogs
For lessons on purity. Where now to look? Who for this will take the heat?

Fish guts, no glory—am I a prophet or a slave? Wait!—forget I asked."
But he answered anyway: "Over a dead gourd you weep and make lament.
Shall I not have pity on so many human lives and creatures too? I tasked
You with giving them a chance to repent; to save their souls you were sent."

And that was the last I ever heard from the Lord. So here I sit in a Joppa bar
Wheedling away my time. A prophet out of work is an odious thing—
Only odd jobs. News of the Temple makes me want and not; being this far
Off I hope he'll leave me be. Little have I left behind; now to nothing cling.

Mary I

The first one birthed is hard to bear;
The older women counselled right,
But none were there that night
To help, so Joseph, for my care
Did all—clear, clean and knot.

His gentle hands were strong;
God's grace to me included him.
Our lamp was small, its light was dim,
Yet in our eyes shone love, a song
Was in my heart. How blessed our lot!

Cattle rustled in the stall; they kept us warm—
My little babe both supped and slept that night—
And when, with dawn and morning light
Led out, the lowing cows looked back to form
A chorus, as if to praise what God had wrought.

My memories now are mixed, the odor of manure,
A glorious luminescence, God's mercy there revealed
To simple shepherds who, with wonder unconcealed
Came to tell the angel's song, in hope and expectation sure
Fulfilled by finding thus the promised Sign. They sought

A manger, found the Child, with me and Joseph, ever mild.

Skywatchers and Scholars

Warned of brigands, we did the last leg up from the Jordan ford at night.
It wasn't just the star we followed; the trail is marked from myriad feet
Trudging through history, theirs and ours. To Babylon enchained, the plight
Of captives, they first came to us; we sent most back long years ago. To meet
Again at Zion's gate their offspring thus seemed strange. "We come in peace,"
I said, and our Chaldean speech was close enough. A coin was further grease;

They let us in. "What do you seek?" an elder spokesman asked. "We seek a king."
A soldier heard and laughed: "They have a 'king'—Caesar's joke—proceed this way."
The palace, unremarkable save for the surly guards, had a courtyard, something
Like a water trough, yet no one offered to stable our camels, even give them hay.
'King' Herod professed no knowledge of a royal birth, just arched his brow
And said his priests told him of Bethlehem the prophecy, urged us to go now

Seek there the child, then bear him directions so he could worship too.
We did not tell him all we knew, that long before the mystery star appeared
In our old library one of us had found a scroll, "God saves" by name. Through
Its tattered pages were mentions of a coming Jewish king, less to be feared
Than welcomed, "a light to lighten the Gentiles," as they call us. Now light
Is what all scholars seek, wisdom, not merely order in the skies at night,

So we read the texts and pondered much, and then one night a light arose
Such as we had never seen. Rotating not, it stayed; then grew and glowed
In the Western sky, brighter to our eyes each night. Balthasar proposed
We take it as the portent of a great event, even as their prophet showed
Would come to Israel. After a year to gaze and think we gathered gear, set
Out along the road and came slowly to that backward land. There we met

With contradictions, so it seemed, to everything one would expect.
But lo, the star grew brighter still, and once we set upon the winding road
To Bethlehem, it slipped down the sky and waited there. You may reject
Our tale, and few would blame you, but hear the rest: the camel load
Of gifts we brought were perfect for a royal babe, but when we found
The very place it was a simple house and shop. We stopped. Around

Was not a single noble dwelling, yet compelled to look within we asked
The carpenter outside if he knew of any royal birth nearby. He raised
His eyes aloft, and palms upraised spoke words we couldn't catch,
Then paused as if to hear some far-off distant sound. Somewhat fazed,
We waited till at last he turned to us and softly said, "The house is small.
I'll bring Mary and the child outside. It will be easier for all."

And so she came, her little one beside her, hand in hand; she smiled
But did not speak. "Many have come," said the carpenter, "but none
So far away as you." Immediately we were struck by her manner, mild
Yet assured as one accustomed to a noble state. She sat next her son
While Joseph fetched hay and water for our camels, bid us also rest.
He looked as any other child might look—except his steady gaze, lest

I forget, which made his face seem wiser than his years. After an hour,
With simple food and drink sufficed, we knew without a doubt some power
Was here, deeper than speech. I nodded to Melchior; he brought the sacks
And we then laid before them gifts, gold, frankincense and myrrh. "Lacks
You may have, but these should help," I said. Mary was overcome with tears,
Joseph astounded—grateful. The little child himself then spoke. Our ears

Distinctly heard the word "*todah,*" and then he smiled. We rose and went
Our way, but in a dream were warned, bypassed that city on a hill, sent
Eastward by another way. Little was as we expected; much more was lent
In wisdom, grace, and gratitude. Something great was coming yet, meant
To heal the world, not as we might imagine, but in a mystery deeper far,
The weak and helpless shall achieve it. We were led to see it by a star.

Mary II

He was an alert and tender child; his first word
Not *mama* but *todah,* he seemed thankful for every smile
And would often cross the room to touch my cheek. Stirred
By the slightest sign of strain or pain he'd come beside awhile,
Hand on my hand and speak his name, *Yeshua.*

What did he then discern? I do not know, but wondered much
And Joseph too, for when the Persians came with gifts he knew,
Nor seemed amazed. Those gifts sustained us for two years, such
Was their munificence, in Mizraim, to which like doves we flew
After the angel's warning in a dream, then prompted, came back home again.

Angels were everywhere in those days, one kind or another,
Sending us here and there for safety, husband, child, and mother.

John the Baptist (a Pharisee Reports)

Popularity was clearly not his aim,
Yet out to the desert people came
To hear him rant, admit their shame.
"A brood of vipers" was the name

He gave to those who taught the Law
Yet failed to hear and do it, rather saw
Their task as to condemn each flaw
In others. That stuck in his craw.

"The voice of one crying in the wilderness" was
All the warrant that he claimed. This much gave pause;
Yet so to quote the Prophet was unjust, because
Isaiah meant our rule restored, with all our laws.

But still the people daily came, conscious, I suppose, of blame
And seeking some release. He washed them with water, named the Name.

A Marginal Man

Just one came back—up and left
The exiled lot with whom he sojourned,
Bound by disease, of kin bereft,
Cast out along with those who spurned
Him well before the spots appeared
To prove indeed what he most feared.

The nine at first all blamed some other,
Then railed at him—a scapegoat, alien vector—
Casting shame upon his bastard race, his mother,
Till tired of that, their hate would turn to hector
Intermittently each other, blaming fate
Or God, in hardened, cynical tones, irate—

Until they met that Man, cried mercy and were healed.
Going giddy thence to priestly confirmation
The tribal scorn of nine resumed, revealed
To him again their ceaseless denigration.
He slowed, then stopped, turned back to One
Whose gracious kindness meant acceptance—life begun.

A Centurion

Out of the crowd at Capernaum stepped a Roman soldier, centurion by rank.
We fell back, thinking he would arrest the Rabbi, yet not so did he speak,
But asked for healing with respect, not for himself but for another, one who sank
Down with mortal illness, not family but a servant, at his home nearby. Meek
In his bearing, not like a commander of men; he said his servant was in great pain
And paralyzed. Would Jesus heal such a one, as before he had, now once again?

Jesus said he would straightway come. The centurion spoke quickly then to plead
That he and his house were unworthy of the Lord; if Jesus would, by word alone
He'd heal the man. Some said he had doubtless something to hide, some need
To cover scandal, but I doubt it. He wasn't the type; you could tell by his tone
"I also am a man under authority," he said—not "with" but "under." Yet none
Could doubt, when to his troops he gave command, that it was promptly done.

His understanding came by faith; he somehow knew with whom he spoke, one able
To accomplish simply by his word what he wished. Many of us gathered 'round were
Curious to see the next miracle, some hoping for a flub, cures to be unstable
Or altogether fail; though sons of Jacob, of signs and wonders' meaning not so sure
As this oppressor. Marking the difference, Jesus dared to speak of it aloud.
He said such *goyim* one day would banquet with our saints. That thinned the crowd.

Descendants of Abraham

Though divided amongst ourselves, still we followed as he walked
From place to place, saying outlandish things, yet healing and teaching
Like a holy prophet. Some pious types believed; others of us balked,
Kept distance, skeptical, or not wanting to be shamed like those reaching
For judgment on adultery at the Temple. To his companions he turned,
Spoke quietly, but I heard—he clearly had the Law bypassed or spurned.

"If you abide in my word," said he, "then you will be my disciples truly—*then* you
Will know the truth, and the truth shall make you free." Some of us demurred;
We learned men knew he had to be a Samaritan or worse, for anyone who
Could say that was no true Jew of any party; even the Sadducees, rest assured,
Would hoot that down from any rabbi. Our credentials needed to be heard:
"We are children of Abraham, never slaves to any man. Make us free? That's absurd."

He seemed to smile. One rolled his eyes. Another laughed: Egypt, Babylon, Romans
Might have another view. My face grew hot when he said, "Whoso sins is slave to sin."
I had told a lie to make a point—did all the time. He knew. In debate he was no man's
Fool, stayed calm when some shouted we were not bastard Jews like him, of doubtful kin,
But actual sons of Abraham. This was our badge of honor. Yet he rebuffed our claim
To be Abraham's sons while refusing Abraham's "yes" to God, and said so to our shame.

Blessed are the Poor in Spirit

So, a master of Torah, honored by the Council,
Need not apply? But a scoundrel like the tax collector
In your story, appearing contrite for his many sins—
His kind of outcast can inherit? Really, Rabbi,
This is outrageous, a calumny against heaven and Temple.
Who would want to be part of such a kingdom
If riff-raff the likes of that man were let in?
Such as they are poor in spirit for good reasons.

Zacchaeus

Being small of stature is no shame;
Poor and orphaned's not to blame;
Some taunt and bully all the same,
Secure in wealth and family name.

These were facts in my young life, recited at night to ease the pain
Of jibes and insults got by day. 'Small' spurs canny, seeks survival;
Skills follow. Doing sums in my head came easy, and right as rain
Was my memory. I found work for both on the tax man's arrival,
And soon moved up the ranks. Loathsome though our daily task,
Offered oversight, I grabbed the chance; took my cut and did not ask.

Revenues rose, the consul approved, and I grew rich—
And so more loathed, not just by my neighbors. No one came
To my house despite my invitations. Friendless, I could lie hurt in a ditch
And no one would help. No synagogue would admit me; the same
For the Temple. Like any Jew I longed to pray—they shut the door.
A plague on my people, I was a tool of the conqueror, nothing more.

I heard about the travelling rabbi, not because he was hard to tax
But for his dealings with the poor and outcast, his healings and wise words.
So when voices in the street noised rumor of his passing by, who could relax?
I had to see for myself. Too thick the crowd, but a flock of birds
Leaving a tree gave me a thought; I ran ahead to a wayside sycamore
He'd pass, and shimmied up to look. I had no hope of more.

The group came into view. I looked in vain for special robes; only that every eye
Was on him marked the man. His raiment dusty like the rest, his sandals plain,
His face not really striking—not what I expected—thus I wondered why
So many followed. But then he looked up at me in the tree and called my name!
"Zacchaeus, come down quickly," said he," for I must stay at your house today."
My ears tingled. On the ground I blurted out, "All I have wronged I will repay!"

Then added, "fourfold! And half of my goods I give to the poor!" No calculation.
Something swept over me like a wind. I just wanted to be clean,
Cleansed by more than water, sensed this Jesus was my chance. In him redemption
Came to me; he sought me out, with such as me was willing to be seen.
When he spoke to the caviling crowd: "Today has salvation come to this house, for *he* is
A son of Abraham"—he meant by faith, not generation. That unsought gift was his

Alone—I didn't see it coming. Lost though I was, I heard the Shepherd's voice, came
Home by a way I never knew. Since chosen by the Lord, my life is not the same.

Mark

In a crowd I usually stay to the back by choice.
In our synagogue in Alexandria they think me shy,
But that night I pressed close, less to hear his voice
Than because I was cold. The beggar had more need than I
Of my cloak, so I gave it. Wrapped only in my linen, feeling
Doubly insecure, when the Temple Guard appeared
And Judas kissed him, I was stunned, mind reeling
At the shame of it. Then, just as we had feared,

They seized him, then began to circle us all, swords drawn.
Peter struck, a mis-aimed blow, cut off somebody's ear;
Then, swiftly stooping, the Lord retrieved it, replaced it on
The injured head and all was as before. One guard drew near
And grasped me by my underclothes, and as I fled, held tight.
I ran as quickly as I could, stark naked, half that awful night.

Between two houses back in town I shivered, helpless till the dawn,
No idea what to do. Then someone saw me, drew near and said,
"Now it's you whose need is more. Here—take back your own."
It was the beggar who spared my shame. Reclothed, I then was led
To shelter underneath the Temple wall, there felt next day the cosmos groan,
Saw sky grow dark at noon, and weeping, touched the trembling stone.

Christ Crucified

On that dry-scabble hill, naked under scorching sun, condemned men are dragged down on wood,
Arms forced akimbo, by sweaty soldiers; rough spikes driven swiftly through their wrists.
Struggle is vain; low moans and pounding hammer blows strike a sordid chord. Each ankle twists
So one large spike will cripple both. Blow on blow, the soldiers curse or jest. At last each cross is stood,
Then dropped into its socket with a sickening thud. Moans of the crucified, echoed by some who watch,
Are countered by cruder curses, accusers, derision much louder than weeping of the grieving few
Who stand back, afraid, though love draws some, inch by inch toward the central cross. Agony not new
In the history of men here too is normal. On the side of that oft-used beam a soldier carves a notch.

Routine torture, routine death. Groaning, gasping, choked up breath, sounds of silence closing, done
By painful fractions as the body sags, that he who ordered nature's laws should not evade them now
Nor scape the curse of human hurt. Passion pent, here spent, love's *extasis in extremis* stalls the sun
But not his torment. Deep darkness dooms; wild angels shriek; the veil is rent. Guilt questions how
The guiltless thus should die; tormentors idly wonder why one prayed they be excused. The lowering sky
Is broken, pierced by prayer: "*Eloi, Eloi! lama sabbacthani!*" The thorn-caught lamb lifts up his final cry.

A Temple Guard

All you asked and more we did. Our cohort of ten
First sealed around the stone with pitch and mortar.
Air-tight it was—no one breathing could still live. Then
We set and kept our watch all night, each of us a porter
To chambers of the dead from whence none return.
Bodies must decay, from them the living may not learn

The fate of souls. We watched all day and saw no sign
Of mischief in the garden. Night fell again; we slept in shifts
Until the first cock crowed; then deep sleep fell on all, the time
Of danger we thought past. Yet something woke me. I saw rifts
Of strange light coming from the tomb. The stone was rolled
Away—that seal could not be broken without tools! A cold

Wind moaned. We jumped up, saw the frightening sight and fled;
Who would stay to wait upon a ghost, or greet the walking dead?

Magdalene Remembers

Desire deep down is never done;
In grief it grows, a gnarled and ghastly thing
Within, it gnaws, grates, burrows into bone.
Before the sun arose I left alone;
I could not wait, but weeping much would bring
Rare perfume to the guarded tomb, would run
Through fearsome soldiers, need far more,
Despite dark death draw near to him I still adore.

Imagine then my anguished heart! The grave was bare,
Stone away and soldiers gone. What have they done?
I cried aloud, then crumpled on a ledge in tears,
Tore my garment, hair distressed; such awful fears
Assailed my soul! Yet one stood by, had heard my cry and come,
Though like a gardener, greater far. None can compare!
His wounded feet I would embrace and pour my ointment out.
I spoke his name and he spoke mine, yet stepped away. No doubt

I wished for more, and yet rejoiced in his "not yet." My Lord! He lives!
Desire transcended, now in him I live whose passion pardons, heals, forgives.

Pentecost I

We gathered there to watch and pray; so bid the Lord.
The upper room was hushed, one voice at a time
Prayed words he taught us, or psalms long stored
In Jewish memories. All kept the fast; hoping for some sign,
When—whoosh!—we heard a roar, like rushing wind, then flame
Appeared above each head! We were aghast. Then came

A torrent of new words, floods of pitched, accented sound.
Our tongues were loosed in praises of our Savior God, naming
Him Lord, his Kingdom come, on all our lips at once were found
Such words as none before had said. A pilgrim crowd remaining
For the harvest feast, Jews dispersed to lands both far and near,
Hearing God praised in each one's foreign speech, were seized by fear.

Some said we Galileans were just drunk, and made some prank or joke
But other ears were opened, hearts aroused, by wonder stirred
Anew to hope. Here were marvels no mocker may revoke,
And also confirmation: into the world we are to go and spread his Word.
Not for us alone, his grace is offered now to every tribe and nation.
Such wideness of his love! In distant lands we'll sing of his salvation

Pentecost II

We came, our lot, from Mizraim,
Most for the Passover,
Then stayed for Shavuot,
Two feasts of obligation.
Though dispersed, we are
Devout, still looking for the Kingdom.

We heard the noise, ran with the crowd
To the court outside an upper room,
Where men were shouting 'Hallelujah'—
Rough Galileans, in our Egyptian tongue
Proclaimed the goodness of the Lord
And his Moshiach! Others from across the world,
From Persia's coast to Pontus, from those dark waters
To the blue Aegean Sea, heard alike the proclamation,
Each in his own adopted alien tongue.

We were amazed. While Judean scoffers mocked
The speakers, saying their speech was drenched in wine,
We could but trust the hearing in our ears. These men
Knew not our foreign speech. Some spoke
Of prayers engulfed in wind and fire,
Of spilling out into the street unconscious
That they praised the Lord in Gentile tongues.

Then stood a man named Simon Peter,
Called for silence and began to speak.
"It's much too early to be drunk," he joked,
"What you have seen and heard
Is of utmost purpose—greatest consequence."

Something like that. The meaning, he went on
To say, is that the Crucified Jesus,
Now raised to life by God, was our Moshiach,
Melech b'a 'Olam, long expected Lord of all,
And showed it from the Scriptures.

Cut to the heart, we repented, each and all
And were baptized by the Twelve—
A busy day that was, with much rejoicing!
Now everywhere we go we sing:

Jesus has come—hallelujah!
God's own son—hallelujah!
Christ our King—hallelujah, hallelujah!
Redeems us from—hallelujah!
The sin we bring—hallelujah!
Unto his Cross—hallelujah, hallelujah!
There washed away—hallelujah!
Like so much dross—hallelujah!
So now we say—hallelujah, hallelujah!
He rose from death—hallelujah!
With every breath—hallelujah!
We sing his praise—hallelujah, hallelujah!
      Amen!

Gamaliel

As the sun rises in the east and goes down in the west,
So does the righteous man of Torah keep a steady course;
He is not shaken from the path of the faithful by rumors
Nor does he waver in the face of sensational claims.
Thus was my Saba's teaching, thus my own.

When from Tarsus that one came to study sacred scrolls
His gifts were noticed from the start; nothing needed
Mention twice, for he kept all he heard or read
Without a scrip or prompt. In discourse shining bright,
He was zealous for all precepts of the Law.

He prayed and worshipped, perfected obedience;
Morning and evening sacrifice were the rhythm of his day.
Others might wander from the way betimes, miss some detail,
But not our Shaul; he set the mark before them all
And might one day, I thought, be a Tzaddik for our times.

I was troubled enough by the Galileans, whose works were such
As are not done except God's hand be in it. Conflicted thus
We let them go. Joseph of Aramathea and Nicodemus too,
Both good men now put from the Council for their support
Of the Nazarene, also give me distraught dreams and little sleep.

Yet none so distresses me as that student now gone
From us, from zeal for the Law to ardent preaching far
Away in synagogues of the diaspora—even, it is said,
To Gentiles in Grecian lands. And yet he conquers,
Wins all sorts of men to his Moshiach. What now to say?

I am dismayed, confused and restless, night and day.

To Timothy: A Postscript

Decline is daily now, infected eyes more dim; discomfort with restraint—
he bears all burdens bravely. We know not when release will come, arrest
His torment. Untroubled by the sentence, his mind is firmly fixed on futures
Other than his own, yours first among them. This postscript to his letter,
mine, not his, comes with his consent, my greeting and confession: I here attest
To his resolve, but also to his resignation. He faces death without complaint,
Content his work on earth is done, as you now have read. I shall remain, better
To attend what follows, loyal to our friend, a *miles Christi* to the end. Yours,

                                                                          Luke

John on Patmos

Exile, for a Jew, is nothing new, my friend; to mend
Our ways was never so appealing as to sin. Thus to rest
At home was not our due, but as captives forced to spend
Sweat, blood, and tears for others' gain, our shame, no guest
Of theirs, but slaves in chains. My exile is instead for Christ, to me
A gift—I am, like Job's messenger, alone escaped to tell thee.

Sufficient word has come: eleven now have passed the test,
Their final witness drenched in blood, some several years ago.
I have been spared—for reasons not yet shown. At his behest
I wait the day, his teaching still digest, his words more deeply know.
Thus on this prison isle I watch and pray, await the moment of my death
When I shall see him face to face, whose love yet summons every breath.

Since last we met, I've seen visions of the end—wonder upon wonder yet
To be and even now—glimpses of heaven, eternal splendor, elders, twenty-four,
Casting crowns of gold beside a crystal sea. A lamb upon his throne was set
Worthy alone to break the seals and read the Book. Signs of judgment still in store,
Yet peace to come when Satan is at last destroyed and Christ alone is king.
All shall bow down before his throne, hail him as Lord, while saints and angels sing.
I dare no more; the rest you'll find within that full, close-written scroll,
Words now not mine but his: let no one tamper, at dreadful peril to his soul.

Miscellaneous Poems

Now I lay me down to sleep,
I pray Thee, Lord,
My soul to keep.
If I should die before I wake,
I pray Thee, Lord,
My soul to take.

Christ on the Cross

I dared not gaze upon his Cross
Lest that anguished face there see
Of One who suffered pain for me.
With guilt I quailed, was at a loss

For words or even thoughts to meet
The horror of that place of shame
Where God my Savior, tortured came
Of his own will to make complete

His saving sacrifice for all
Who turn repentant eyes on him,
Then grateful, loving, take him in
Heart, soul and mind. Now I recall

The beauty of his grace each day
So meet his gaze, there hold and stay.
Who will not own him on the tree
The risen Lord has not set free.

The Cross

Christ's cross of glory once I fled, blind to all but shame.
His thorn-crowned, bleeding, pain-wracked face
Too ugly seemed, for comfort vain; his saving grace
Most surely came with Easter morn, I thought, no other claim
Between the last, most sacred meal and life above
Made sweet account, or beauty showed.
                        "But what of love?"

That question I'd not asked; the voice fell on my inner ear
While I was shuffling by the Cross, not looking up, as was my wont.
It slowed me down; I paused, then stopped short near the font,
Turned back from exit with slow steps. Drawing near
Again I trembled, stood beneath that ancient image stark, the Cross
Above the altar. Looking till my vision blurred, I knelt to mourn my loss.

I loved Easter morning as a child, praised the open tomb in song;
Now first I face the death that conquered death, so also to his Cross belong.

Blessed are the Meek

The tap, tap, tap of roofers, high up next door
Mixes with their chatter—Spanish I can't follow,
Mingles with laughter, drifts down, and more;
Now and then one bursts into song, as if a swallow
Or warbler had settled here to nest.

I rake my leaves and listen to these men at work,
Aware that but two blocks away,
Drinking on a porch, lounging men would rather shirk
Than any ladder climb, are paid to stay
At home: two worlds apart, two views of life and rest.

A cell phone shrieks—in English speaks: "this is a test."

Quaecumque sunt Vera
for Rhiannon

Whatsoever things are true—though some find nonesuch,
Whatever honorable—ask not of elites or noble rank,
Whatever just—look not to lawyers, nor judges much,
Whatever pure—find if you can and then God thank
Who made all things beautiful—praise him to the end;
Whoever proves most gracious, choose him for your friend.

Rejoice always, even when hope seems lost,
And in your gentleness, as the Apostle says, let
Gratitude be your reason. Don't overcount the cost,
But be content to trust in God. With his peace set
Deep in your mind, despite much outward strife
You'll never be dismayed, or lose your joy of life.

Those who nothing of your calm now share will thereby see
Something beyond their ken, that nonetheless may be
      —also for them.

On Handel's *Coronation Anthem*
(*Christus Rex*, 2021)

A monarch? Now they use some other name—
President, Premier, Chairman, Leader—
Imperious still, though each and all proclaim
A reign more worthy than the last. Let the reader
Hear what Samuel told the ancient Jews:
The one you think the answer when you choose
May tempt you soon enough to second guess, again
To wish your choices back, but all in vain.

Divided we are. Who now can feel such general joy,
The thrill when all as one acclaim, 'God save the King'?
No Zadok priest, no prophet Nathan now inform the *hoi
Poloi* that God concurs; no Handel choirs men's hearts to sing
With hope renewed for bruised and broken lands.
We dream toward a future King, to be one day in better hands.

Advent I
(Zech. 12:1–9)

The word that Zechariah heard, the word he spoke,
Was from the Lord, a word of warning yet of hope
Amidst the troubles then and still to come, when heavy yoke
And tyrants' rod alike shall snap beside Mt. Olive's slope,
When there the final crack of doom appears
As on that day the sovereign feet return to stand
Upon the holy Mount. Asunder it shall split, and any other fears
Seem small. All then shall wait upon the Lord's command.

We who look toward the coming King in this our troubled day
Have time to look upon his promised signs, to watch and pray;
Through warfare, tumult, pestilence, storm, travail—
Still worse, the self-willed madness, reason's small avail
For nations in denial—despite these things should keep our peace,
Store treasure far above the fray, look up for true redemption and release.

Advent II
(Luke 3:1–6)

Unexpected, unsuspected, the stranger came
From well beyond the pale, unkempt, a wild man
In animal skins. Such was his sudden fame
That people from the city, curious, without a plan
Trekked out to see and hear him say
"Repent! The Kingdom of Heaven is at hand."
Again he cried, "Repent and be baptized this day;
Even now the one God sends is on his way!"

His urgent plea was unadorned, save for phrases
Plucked from the Prophet. These struck a chord
In many hearts. The faithful came in droves, his famous
Preaching first to hear, and hearing, to accord.
Immersed in Jordan's waters at the ford,
Contrite and grateful, some acted on his word.

Advent III
(Luke 3:7–18)

Whether his preaching was good news
Depended on truth in the inward parts.
Some came to judge—
Claimed the Covenant but veiled their hearts.
Undeceived, the wild man spoke his mind:
"Brood of vipers" wasn't what they liked to hear,
Nor what came next. Whereas they hoped to find
Approval of some kind, exposure led to fear.

To be ready for the Kingdom of the Lord
Is not to know but *do* the deeds which show
Repentance isn't only words; a sword
Must sever worldly lusts, and though
It costs we must restore, past harms repair,
And practice love to all, so in his Kingdom share.

Advent IV
(Luke 1:26–38)

No restlessness of heart, but steady
On from dawn till dwindling sun
She worked, prayed, and learned. Readied
For each morrow thus, she also waited for the One
To come, in patience, son of David sent to set
His people free—a lasting, final, true release.
Such was her life; she pondered much, yet
When her daily work was done she slept in peace.

Then the angel spoke. She was of course surprised,
But not dismayed. His gracious regal greeting met
No protocol she knew; yet once apprised
The Spirit now drew nigh, she didn't fret,
But guileless and alert received the Word,
With heart and soul embraced her Sovereign Lord.

Christmas Eve, 2021
(Isaiah 9:2–7)

Deepest down dark doubts, no daybreak shows, and yet a rooster crows.
Dull despair with lists of failures skirts the pit, may even flirt with death,
And yet a candle burns. Somewhere somehow someone knows
That light is coming, that healing, hope, new life and breath
Shall raise up scattered, broken bones. Though no one lives
Without some slender gleam, some hint of morning light
Beyond the bleak and fitful shades of night, one who gives
Another day a chance shall find that dawn has pierced the night.

For those who dwell in darkness drear, clear light now shines,
For those who wander, lost in wilderness within, a path appears;
It leads to stable straw, the odor of manure. Humility refines
Our sense of worth; we come to see at last above our fears
The face of Love. Wonderful his counsel, marvelous his might:
Where feeble fathers failed, his perfect peace portends true Light.

Nod: A Child's Hebrew Lesson

Nod in Hebrew: meaning 'wander,' swift or plod;
Literal, figural, appears as noun and verb.
That Cain goes wandering in the land of Nod
Connects the dots, both senses of this little word.

Though baleful was his exile curse,
Not to get the nod from God is worse;
To get lost in the desert that one fears
Is lesser consequence, despite the tears.

Wherever you find yourself on earth,
Of empty trails there is no dearth.
The one who wanders rarely alters
The wilderness in which hope falters.

To be a pilgrim differs, to walk while having
Hope of *final* destination. *Halach,* the verb
Invokes the noun, 'life-changing way of living'.
Who walks with God is never lost. Absurd
Though men may think a pilgrim's plight,
(who walks by faith and not by sight),
Through threats by day and harms by night
His path is sure, God's word his light.

On Psalm 119:105
for my grandchildren

Wisdom, a quality of mind and heart,
Ingathered sense, a kind of art
As apt to reason as to rule,
Is more than what you learn at school.

And so with understanding: when
Discernment probes past page and pen
As good as courage under fire
Is thinking through each quick desire.

Knowledge is best when serving ends
Beyond our own, in gifting friends,
And not as means to wealth and power,
But thankfulness, each day, each hour.

All work together while we pray
To One whose leading lights our way.

Persuasion
for Eowyn

I once had a friend with a cat
whose affection was likewise ambiguous.
It had a way of presenting gifts,
chipmunks and mice, laid at the door.
These were, quoth my friend, sweet tokens,
Offerings, feline courtesies,
furry little corpses, dripping blood.
To see such offerings as gift I thought naive,
a kind of dead-letter rhetoric,
trophies without taxidermy,
demonstrating utter independence;
a cat can always provide its own lunch.
Such 'presents' were actually brute negotiation;
that cat wanted sardines, caviar, gravy,
and was pressing its case like a Brooklyn thug.

Yang's Gift—an antique snuff bottle,
painted from the inside
for Cara Grace

This lady, under her golden gown
Wears robes of azure, soft as down.
Her feet unbound, she walks with ease,
No emperor's whim shall ever please.

Hers is not a helpless sport,
Unwilled compliance in the royal court,
But high on a mountain path she goes,
Rings on her fingers, bells on her toes.

Reviewing my Latest Chinese Banquet
epistle to my grandchildren

Confucius, who relished his scorpions fried
Had too many helpings, it seems.
His joints and his chest were gravely tried
With pains and contractions extreme—
Accordingly, laying himself to rest,
Thought modest consumption of scorpions best.

The eel of the swamp and rice paddy mud
Is a "delicacy fit for kings."
This largest leech in the marshy flood
Is cooked when cut into wriggly rings,
Then served with a sauce so hot and red
It sends you home tossing and turning to bed.

The rat dines on garbage in every clime,
But in China is harvested back.
When boiled and shredded in "sauce sublime"
Or sautéed with garlic (for those with the knack)
Revenge on the rodent's a tasty treat
And the juice that remains may be swallowed neat.

Of all the refinements of Cantonese art
Sea-cucumber's surely the coup.
But the botanical ruse gives one's tongue a start,
For no vegetable dish or edible soup
Can be made from this slug of the ocean floor.
Its slime's irreducible. Have some more?

The snake I usually save for last,
Or the fish still alive in the dish,
And the puppy and cat are such a blast
(Less exotic than one might wish).
How I'd like some strong tea, a gallon or three
To wash down this banquet in honor of me.

And soon I am staggering home to bed
To sleep off another waist-full day,
Then work and wait till next I'm fed.
Preserve me, Lord, I pray!
Such kindness I can scarce abide;
Tonight I'd—frankly—rather hide.

Everyday Valentines

Tonight there are roses on the table, pink,
A bag of Swiss chocolates on one side,
A bottle of Tempranillo on the other. To think
These gestures are but custom fails far wide
Of the mark, for the pair that shall dine
Here have lived and loved for forty years,
Their laughter in the kitchen more true a sign
Of love than such mere tokens; even tears
In this abode transcend occasion, embrace
The greater good of grateful sharing, face to face.

Snowdrift
a song

A thousand eyes think I am theirs
When I drink wine,
But they fade away when I start to think
On your voice and mine.
Ah, but my love's now quiet, silent
As snowdrift's hush,
And my love is like unto
A berry on the blackthorn bush.

Of Life to Come

If you could see beyond this page
Then each shaped word would fail to tell—
If we could hear beyond this space
What past or future bells might knell,
These notes would lend no further grace
Much less one fear assuage, dispel—
If each could know beyond this hour
Our love of life itself would sink,
Annul each joy, unmake the flower
In perfumes of our pleasure. Think!
Of rosebuds then who'd ransom some,
Reaching for life that's still to come?

Recipe for Insomnia

When restless mind at night conspires
Against the sweet release of sleep,
My fretful memory then requires
A list of promises to keep
Much longer than in fact I can
Fulfil in my diminished span
Of nights and days; I then arise
And ponder what before me lies.
The trouble is I can't see much
But blurry shapes; I'm not in touch
With crystal balls or clairvoyance.
So what's to do, I humbly pray,
But crack the fridge to find, perchance,
Some snacks to keep night thoughts at bay?

About Kalypso

All places I have been, that I have loved,
Seem unreal, equally far,
Their air grown thin—
slight as perfume on the seven seas
Where once she swam.
Once, and not more.

Ten thousand fish still whirl dizzily
In her wake, and, dazed upon this shore,
I lie now, wasted, spent,
Like seaweed on the rocks,
A castaway.

Telemachus

Rounding these reefs, the storm-tossed track seemed long enough.
Thinking me home, woke a stranger in a stranger's land.
Then overplayed my hand. Daft. Who could now that time rerun
Or yet its fears command? To build new vessels, leave old plans,
Might find another way. Release. So bid what dragons will to sleep.
If slowly turns the wheel of stone, more slowly mend these shards of bone.

Hark!
Over the sea wall furies moan;
Odysseus wanders, far from home.

La petite voisine d'Essoyes
homage à Renoir

Your fingers touch each petal, miss,
As "ti oiseaux—ou papillon";
The light that falls through leafy boughs
Upon your arms and breasts
Like silk—enfolds you, gold and green.
"Elle est belle, et elle est pûr,"
He said; je suis d'accord.
He loves to paint you, clothed or not.
Because his love is art
His looks caress, his paint-brush sets you free.
When I grow tall I wish to glow,
A rose among the lilies white,
Like you; I want to be
As beautiful and pure,
As comely, and to bathe in light.
If he is not too frail or old,
Perhaps Papa then will paint me too,
As here and now, with tender touch,
So happy in our garden,
He is painting you.

October

Laid on his arm, her hand was warm,
Her fingers smooth, aglow like pearls.
He looked into her waiting eyes
And met a gaze as old as time;
He smiled assent. They rose and went,
Then lay once more in passion spent.

The night outside was still and clear;
A frost was on the lawn. Both slept,
Entwined like vines until the dawn.
Light shimmered in the orchard leaves;
It shone like diamonds on the grass.
They woke, kissed twice, and rose at last.

Thus ageless memory, cherished, gleams
And joy finds reason, rhyme and dreams.

Misreading

I knew that poet once. Dark,
Roiling locks, thick browed
And brown eyes peaceful as a doe.
Noticing much, he counseled nothing.

He knew the enthymemes unclasped,
The nape-hairs translucent
On many a graceful neck;
Liked them best in lamplight.

Silent likewise. In love he bade
Them speechless, that they might
The better listen to his moving hands,
Their own soft, quickening breaths.

They came in lissome numbers,
Silent readers of an ancient text
That rose, swelled, surged
Within their aching loins and breasts

And died away in waves of yearning,
Burning softly, like his lamp.

Confession

When most aware of wrong and sin,
Of bridling anger in my heart,
Injustice, bias on some part
If not the whole, a look within
Finds ample causes there for sorrow,
These faults my own. No need to borrow
Offences from abroad to chide,
My own disordered soul to hide.

For I am seen, and thoughts confirm
Your Word within my soul reproves.
Lest I forgiveness forfeit, mercy spurn,
Retain the stain your blood removes,
O keep me from presumptuous sin,
From judging others you would win.

Just a Toast at Twilight

Fireflies flit softly up and down our lawn,
Dancing their lady loves to music I can't hear,
A kind of light pavan. Tree frogs, keen to spawn,
Sound urgent notes, high in the oaks, more near
The changing sky. Across the bay I see four deer
Descending to the water, silently from here.

Above them all a sunset weaves its fleeting gold,
An amber glow through purple clouds, and still
The breeze is soft, the jasmine sweet. Though I am old
Sparks, songs and sighs my senses fill.
A mile beyond some cattle graze upon a hill;
One calls her calf. I smile and lift my glass—
       let nothing spill.

Somnium

The old book at last set down, eyes blurred with tears,
From doubt and wonder worn, weary, as wakened fears
Crowd in upon the heart and mind of one who nears
His day of reckoning, the aged reader fell asleep.

Prelude or premonition, upon his inward eyes a dream
Crept softly, light diffused. He stood beside a gentle stream—
Its place he knew not—and on his clouded gaze a gleam
Of amber light shone down to show a chalice next the deep.

He stopped, uncertain, then stooped to grasp the cup.
It burned his touch, he let it drop; and dared not pick it up.
What sort of thing is this? Is not this a goblet made to sup
Like any other? His hand still burned; the cost of error steep.

And yet he could not leave it there, so with his boot he dug a hole
And with an aspen bough he pushed it in. That strangely took a toll
On waning strength. Though short of breath he added moss, let roll
A nearby stone to cover all, and stepping back, began to weep.

Then years rolled by, it seemed, and he returned unto that very spot
Beside the flowing stream. He saw the stone close by and thought
That he would lift and look to see what time had wrought.
Only an imprint in the clay remained to taunt and haunt his sleep.

September Rain

All nature loves a gentle rain.
Rose blossoms lift, sage leaves cup,
As if to sup, each drop a gain
In jade-like green. As we look up,
See warblers plump with ruffling wings
And hear the singing rainfall brings
To all and sundry feathered things,
Wee wrens and finches follow suit,
From limb to limb in fresh pursuit
Of softer bark and dampened shells
To find a favored treat. Their music swells;
Each song their glad thanksgiving spells.

Bittersweet

Just where the old split-rail graveyard fence
Enters a thicket hedge, wild plum and cherries,
A vine grows through summer in secret, hence
Only with frost and fallen leaves appear its berries,
Orange shells, split, show ripe red seeds, for birds
A winter harvest visible through snow, and sweet,
For humans toxic, fatal to the very young. No words
Appear but such as strewn and scattered stones repeat.

And yet our mothers sent us out to gather sprays,
Décor for the mantle, for tables at Thanksgiving.
Lovely, but dangerous, they became mainstays
Of festal mood and cheer, a sign among the living:
Though winter may be hard, its blizzards unforgiving,
There's provision for all creatures yet, bread and beauty giving.

Azura

Azura. Blue as deepest sky above,
Blue as your eyes. The lake below reflects
That farther light, absorbs, and thus deflects
The brilliance we can't bear. A cooing dove
Prefers to hide in deeper green of tall oak trees
Whose outer boughs like emeralds shine.
Responding, like to like, a gentle chime,
Aeolian, chords with birdsong in the breeze.
The dappled sunlight dancing on our lawn
Yields yet more shades of green, a harmony
Of tones. Thus colors, sounds, a symphony
Compose, all moved by sunlight brushed upon
The canvas of this small garden walled in stone.
Here cardinals sing, monarchs swoop in play,
Squirrels chase and scold, as if to say—
You are not by yourself—no creature is alone.

Snow Geese

Among the pleasures of autumn, I count
Splitting and stacking firewood in ricks;
Raking leaves, maple and oak, which mount
In heaps for children to leap and laugh; and even tricks
Of squirrels to rob me of pecans they have found
Green in the tree, before they fall to ground.

Yet I am charmed still more by a spectral sound
Of snow geese, far above in lofty chorus,
So high to me invisible. Year after year I have found
Their marking of the waning season for us
As lovely as the changing hues of leaves—
October's blossoms, dancing in the breeze.

The world they leave behind, below, shall yield to snow,
Surrender all. Yet they'll pass by in spring, I know.
For now, though bitter winter winds may blow,
Their cries still echo while the embers glow,
Till one fine morning, far above the budding trees
Their song will reach me, gardening, happy on my knees.

Migrating Water Birds

A flotilla fair of pelicans, gleaming white, had settled on our bay,
Surrounded there by wheeling gulls, who gather not to play
But scavenge what they can from others' fruitful labors;
Brigands of the beach, they brunch on scraps and unmeant favors
Of bigger creatures, complaining all the while that what they munch
Lacks savor, salt or seasoning, is mushy, or too hard to crunch.

Two days on that crowd is gone to fish another shore,
Their vacancy leaves quiet space, the inlet then more
Tranquil till a pair of loons appears; this year I heard
Them first, as often is, one calling to the other bird
To say, "I'm near—are you?" Then, to form quite true,
I saw both dip, fly under deeper water as they do

To catch their minnows far beneath. They travel long in flight,
And fishing well apart by day, float side by side at night,
Go not in flocks, but pair for life. That seems to me just right,
Who from my clifftop chair attend, as much by listening as by sight.

Arc of the Covenants

Arca, just a box, but large enough to hold
The seeds of life within its wood.
Another, smaller box would hence enfold
The words of life, which long have stood
The storms and ravages of time.

Though both are lost, what they once held
Endures, breathes yet, engenders life.
The arc which shone and promise spelled
Returns despite our ceaseless strife
And still appears above, a sign.

The Architect of Word and Works presides.
While ages come and go, he turns his scroll
To yet another place; as one more life subsides
Into the great abyss, as epochs roil and roll,
Provides another marker, casts his line.

For every life, within his Law or not,
There is a limit set; measurements made
Before our ken establish every lot,
Each mortal span. Thus, as one still stayed
I know a lesser box is coming—mine.

Yet this too, by his grace is transit.
For those who in his promise trust
Are bound for life as mercy grants it;
Though darkness fall, frail flesh must
Then be raised: completing his design.

www.ingramcontent.com/pod-product-compliance
Lightning Source LLC
Chambersburg PA
CBHW071153090426
42736CB00012B/2321